Your Journey With Grief

A Space to Express Yourself
And
Keep the Legacy of Your
Loved One Alive

By Monica L Morrissey

James 1:3
Because you know that the testing of your faith produces perseverance.

Your Journey With Grief

A Space to Express Yourself
and
Keep the Legacy of your Loved one Alive

By Monica L. Morrissey

Copyright

made
with
love

For all who are

experiencing grief

A Note from the Author

My first book, *Dimes from Heaven, How Coins and Coincidences Helped Me Discover My Life as an Empath* came from my soul. It was a journey within myself that I hadn't planned to do. It was as much of a surprise to me as it was to many of my friends and family. I originally thought I was writing a ten page cool story that I hoped would be passed on to my kids and Grandkids. But, when I started writing, it was like spirit stepped in to assist me in my journey with my grief. The door to Heaven seemed to open and help me share my story with the world. I was honored that people enjoyed reading my story.

More Dimes from Heaven, A Journey to Self-Publishing was filled with more dimes but also other messages that were sent to me during my writing journey. Each chapter guides the reader to write their book to publish their story. I hope it encourages people to share their story with the world.

Once Upon a Dime, Heaven is Talking to Us. Do You Know How to Listen?, my third book, also had Divine intervention. Spirit guided me with more coincidences and helped my readers understand how to tap into this spiritual (not religious) energy in a way that would support them during their journey here on earth. The universal law of attraction and signs of the after-life brewed in all of the stories.

Now, I want you to have the gift of writing about your grief to discover peace within your soul and feel a bit closer to Heaven.

Monica

Connect with me:
Facebook http://www.facebook.com/groups/dimesfromheaven
Instagram @dimefromheaven
Website https://www.monicalmorrissey.com/

Dear Reader,

I am honored you are here right now. Grief is such a journey and it seems to be a continuous non-stop reminder that life is such a precious gift. When someone leaves this world, the pain left behind is a reminder to us all still here that life can be taken at any moment in time.

Writing sure helped sooth my aching heart. Although writing won't bring our loved ones back, I do know that it helps us process our grief and helps to be able to connect with the other side. Writing also helps us hold on to the memory of our loved ones. I am grateful that my grandchildren and great grandchildren are always going to know about my dime stories. I hope they feel a deep connection to those in Heaven.

Just as how you experience grief is different for everyone, feel free to use this journal in any way you wish. The pages are filled with ideas but there are also blank pages to use as you wish.

My hope for you is to have a space to express some of your feelings that you may be holding onto so that you can live the rest of your life with more peace and joy. Our life is such a gift and I want you to be able to enjoy each moment.

My other hope for you is that maybe you'll unlock the door to Heaven with your writing. The Universe loves you to write down what you want so that it truly knows and understands your desires.

I've been there. I've been deep in the darkness of grief and I know how painful it is. There is no way out. Grief shows up in many events in our lives-not just death. For example, we can experience grief as parents when our kids move out or we might experience grief when getting a divorce. Whatever you are grieving, this journal is a safe place to write about your feelings and then move forward in your life.

For each question, just put pen or pencil to paper and see what happens. Spirit loves to work through your pen and when you start writing, ideas appear sometimes out of nowhere. Enjoy the process.

Here is an example of this. The prompt I was writing about was "I lied". I could sit and think about it but when I put pen to paper, what appeared didn't seem to come from my brain. It came from deep within my soul, hidden in my subconscious. Here is what I wrote:

"I lied. For sure. Without a doubt. I didn't know how to speak the truth. I didn't think anyone would believe me. I thought people would be angry if they heard the truth.

I didn't think it was safe to say it out loud. I thought that people weren't ready to hear it. I thought if I lied, then they would believe the lie. But, in truth, they all knew the truth. They could not only feel it but they could see it in my eyes. They knew I was lying even though I didn't want them to know.

It was the elephant in the room that I wasn't ready to talk about. It would mean I would have to face the truth.

How would I ever be able to do that? What would help me be able to face it? I can't believe this is happening. Especially now, of all the times in my life. Why couldn't it happen next week, after I have been able to talk about it and accept it?

I can't lie. I don't know how to do it. Internally, I am sick and my body listens to everything my mind thinks. Why did I ever think I would be able to do this? I couldn't do it even when I tried. I ended up blurting the truth and apologizing. Lying is not something I can do. I think because it hurts so much when it happens to me. It cuts into my heart and I can't seem to cut into someone else's heart. It's not how I am built. It isn't inside me to do that."

When I had put pen to paper, I had no idea what would appear. That magic happens when we let go and allow our pen to flow.

As with many things in life, there are times to question "the norm". For decades in America, most have believed that grief is to be healed by working through the five stages of grief developed by Kubler-Ross. But, what if this wasn't true? We actually never "heal" from grief. It appears throughout the rest of our lives. Sometimes we just ignore it or don't know what to do with it. Sometimes we get stuck in it and can't seem to get out. But, there is a way to live everyday heart-centered and carrying on the legacy of those who are in Spirit.

Kubler-Ross created those stages for people who were facing their own death, not the death of a loved one. David Kessler, who worked with Kubler-Ross for many years clarifies this in his book, *Finding Meaning*. He states that pain is inevitable but suffering is optional. He instead tries to find meaning in the experience. May you find clarity and a deep sense of peace as you write.

An excerpt from *Once Upon a Dime Heaven is Talking to Us. Do You Know How to Listen?*

Chapter 2 Experiencing Grief- Beyond the Five Stages

"Sometimes I forget how rich I am. My hot water works on a dime, my a/c works when I need it to. I can go to any grocery store and purchase what I please to eat. I have a clean kitchen to cook in. I have a clean shower to bathe in...sometimes I forget I'm beyond blessed." –Author unknown

If there is one thing in life people can be sure of is that they are going to die. Eventually, the body we were given at birth will fade away and many will wonder, "Does this mean I am gone forever?" I've wondered about why I am here on earth for so long that now I don't know what it would be like to not wonder about my life.

When I was growing up and a person died, the person was erased like hitting the delete button on a computer. They were gone and there was nothing else to discuss. We did not celebrate their life and we didn't even express how sad we were that they were gone. My family didn't discuss death before it happened and we definitely didn't talk about the possibility of someone else dying. I barely heard stories about my Grandfather who died two weeks before my birth.

The most well-known stages of grief in America were developed by Kubler Ross in 1969 (I was one year old!) and these would become so ingrained into our society that fifty years later they are still accepted (in America) as the only way to grieve. Some are guided to "heal" by "moving through" the stages. Why are we using such an outdated system? I'm not still using the telephone system from the sixties, why would I use an outdated psychological process for dealing with a major life event?

What most people might not know is that Kubler-Ross and David Kessler designed the five stages to be used for people who were facing their own death. They didn't create them to use after a person died.

The five stages developed by Kubler-Ross & Kessler are the following: 1. denial 2. anger 3. bargaining 4. depression 5. acceptance. A person who lost a loved one is made to feel that if you dealt with these feelings, eventually you would feel better. As anyone who has experienced the deep loss of their loved ones knows, grief is not something that goes away. Losing someone affects us for the rest of our lives.

I remember when my mother died. I definitely wasn't in (1)denial- she was gone. How could I deny that? I was (2)angry. I was angry that she wouldn't go get help when she knew she was sick. How was anger going to help me feel better? It wouldn't bring her back so it was pointless to be angry. (3)Bargaining? What was I to bargain for? She was gone and there was nothing to do but live without her. The (4)depression didn't catch up to me for years after her death. My father most definitely experienced depression and wondered why he was left behind. He was ready to go be with her. My depression hit later on when I realized that I never had the relationship with my mother that I wanted. (5)Acceptance seemed to be difficult at first but with time, there was nothing else to do but create a new life without my mother.

David Kessler added two new stages to the five stages - shock and finding meaning. The shock felt by an unexpected death can rock us to our core. When this happens to me I feel like time stops and nothing else in life matters anymore. It's like I'm watching a movie and I am one of the characters. I get angry easily and can't seem to focus on anything. Nothing else seems important. After the initial paralyzed feeling, then it's time to create a new way to live without the physical presence of the person.

It is difficult to describe but there is this overwhelming, unbearable feeling, especially if the death is a surprise. Brene Brown nails the emotion in her new book, Atlas of the Heart. She calls it anguish and this is her description," Anguish is an almost unbearable and traumatic swirl of shock, incredulity, grief, and powerlessness." It feels like life is so out of my control that there is no way to get through the experience. Since we all do get through it, I wonder what the lasting effects are of those moments when we first learn about a death. The trauma stays in our bones and radiates within our bodies. It's what I felt as a baby inside my mother's womb, but as a child I didn't have the resources to process the grief.

One thing that I believe is missing from the stages is anxiety. When someone dies, I immediately think, "Oh no, what if I die? What if someone close to me dies?" I go to this place where everything is scary. What if I have cancer? What if I have heart disease? What if someone I love gets into a car accident? Everyday becomes scarier and scarier. I have to remind myself that each day is not promised. I have to remind myself of the value in being alive and that our time on earth is determined by a greater power than me. I am able to take steps to create a healthy life but, ultimately, when it is time to go, we all leave this earth and transition back to our spirit form.

What if there was another way to experience grief? What if there weren't linear stages to work through like we were attending school and trying to graduate? What if through our loss we found strength and a deep connection to something beyond human explanation- like universal spirit or our own soul? What if we allowed our grief to express itself every single time it appeared? And then, we took time to remember the love of the person who was gone. What if we found meaning through the experience or decided to find meaning in our loved ones' life? And decided to embrace that part of them in our own life?

I've noticed a difference in how people experience death depending on their belief in God. When I speak of God, I'm not talking necessarily about a specific religion or a man up in the sky controlling everything. What I mean is there is a universal, invisible connection to "something" and that "something" is "out there" and "in here". "Out there" includes many mysteries like nature, the solar system and all of life. How else are we able to explain how a tree grows or how animals live or how the moon circles the earth? The "in here" is a feeling within us that feels love and connection. Our hearts are alive and connected to "something". This connection with God or universal intelligence or whatever we want to call it is so much more than we are able to put into words and it requires trust; which I call faith. If we allow this connection to "something", then our life experiences are filled with awe and wonder.

There are two other models of grief that may help more than the original stages. J. William Worden's four tasks of grieving (from his book Grief Counseling and Grief Therapy) and Thomas Attig's grief process (from his book How We Grieve: Relearning the World) introduce us to a different perspective. Worden's tasks are not linear in fashion and may be done for the rest of your life. There is no graduation in your grief and it is acceptable to continue your journey using these.

The four tasks are 1. Accept the Reality of the Loss 2. Process Your Grief and Pain 3. Adjust to the World Without Your Loved One 4. Find a Way to Maintain a Connection to Your Loved One. These tasks allow for a lot of emotions during the process. And, personally speaking, I love number four as that is what has helped me the most. Grief and death have changed my life in such incredible ways that I never would have imagined.

Thomas Attig's process includes some of the similar tasks to Worden's. Thomas suggests the following: 1. Changes in the Physical World 2. Changes in Relationships with Others Still Living 3. Changes in Perspective on Time 4. Changes in Spiritual Grounding 5. Changes in Relationship with the Deceased 6. Changes in Identity.

Both of these models allow you to stay connected to your loved one. This is the key to experiencing life after loss. Without this connection, the pain and suffering can be overwhelming. As David Kessler states in his book, Finding Meaning, "Pain is inevitable. Suffering is optional." David also wrote, "When we move through pain and we release it, we fear there will be nothing, but the truth is, when the pain is gone, we are connected only in love."

Recently, I was chatting with a co-worker who found meaning in her friend's death. Tracy shared with me that her lifetime friend, Missy, passed away due to cancer and because of this, Tracy had a whole new outlook on life. Tracy said that the family was not having a "funeral" but they were going to have a Celebration of Life instead. She explained that Missy was full of life and that, along with their tears, they were going to remember all the great things about Missy. Tracy wasn't going to wear black or a dark color; her outfit would be bright and colorful - just like Missy's personality. This would remind her of the love she had for her dear friend.

Then, Tracy went on to explain how she had changed her thoughts after the death of her friend. She realized that we aren't promised to live forever and that life is very short. Tracy was going to think about food differently. Instead of filling her body with junk, she made the decision to treat her body better so that she might live a long life! She was going to be grateful for each day that she was alive.

I felt Missy's presence in the room with us. Tracy's love for her friend helped Missy in the Spirit world be able to share her energy. Tracy's goosebumps were all I needed to know that her friend appreciated everything about Tracy. Missy's legacy lived on in Tracy; forever changing the way Tracy viewed her life.

I, just like Tracy, have learned to live life differently now that I understand that this life is not guaranteed. Before we journey on together, let me preface the remainder of this book by saying that I am not a grief expert. If you need help from a professional, please get help. What I am going to share with you is what I learned about life and the possibility of an afterlife while I experienced grief. This book may not be the book for you to deal with deep pain. What this book does do is give the reader a different way to look at death and learn how to connect to a spiritual world - one that I discovered while searching for answers about death. It's a different way to live and I hope you enjoy the stories.

The magic of connecting with our loved ones seemed impossible to me at first. It's in my gratitude practice and belief in "something" that allowed me to live my life each day as though everything is a miracle. I sort of believed in signs before my parents died, but through my grief, I learned how deep this connection is. I also experienced the magic of connecting where my relationships (with my mother especially!) were healed and I let go of the pain and emotions of anything that didn't serve me.

Loss and grief show up in our life in many ways, not only death. It showed up in my life when my kids moved out, when I switched jobs or even when letting go of physical objects. My grief for my mother was very different from losing my father. With my mother, my grief was for never having a strong mother-daughter relationship. For my father, my grief was more about both of my parents gone. I was too busy making plans and taking care of their estate. These feelings of grief appeared years later and I didn't exactly know how to handle all of my feelings.

In this book, you are going to hear stories about people connecting with their loved ones in the spirit world- which I think is magical. Through my search for understanding grief and the signs of after-life, I am forever grateful to know these people and for them sharing their stories of deep connections to their loved ones. They are magical and most definitely show a connection to "something" more than we may ever fully comprehend. They guide us along this journey of life and most likely may spark changes in your life that you may not have expected. When we look beyond our physical world into this invisible layer of love, our hearts feel better and our lives are richer.

Once Upon a Dime is available for purchase on Amazon, Barnes and Noble and any bookstore.

Want to write more? Join my Online Writing group- Soul Writer's Unite! Contact me for more information at monicalmorrissey@gmail.com

"In heaven, we can see you...We can feel you...We know your pain, your tears, but we feel no pain or tears ourselves...There are no bodies here...there is no age...The old who come...are no different than the children...No one feels alone...No one is greater or smaller...We are all in the light...the light is grace...and we are part of...the one great thing."

by Mitch Albom

The First Phone Call from Heaven

"Understanding Death as a Transition...

I believe, at our core, we are all energy. Energy cannot be made. It cannot die. It can only be transformed. When we die, I believe our energy becomes free from our physical forms (i.e. our bodies) and transforms into spirit. As such, our loved one's energy is always with us and it's always around us."

By Cathleen Elle

Read more in her book,
Shattered Together
A Mother's Journey From Grief to Belief
A Guide to Help You Through Sudden Loss

Your Grief Permission Slip

"You have every right to find your own way through grief, even if your way looks wildly different from that of others. There is no generic advice or timeline that you need to follow. No one has the right answers, no matter how wise they may be or how well versed in grief they are. ~Monica Ten-Kate

I, Monica L. Morrissey, give you, the reader, permission to experience his/her/their grief in whatever way he/she/they would like.

Signed *Monica L. Morrissey 6/11/23*

Kubler-Ross wrote about the 5 stages of grief in the book, *On Death and Dying*. But, did you know that she was "actually writing about the experience of facing one's own death, not the death of someone else." ?~Ruth Davis Konisberg

Find out more in her book, *The Truth about Grief*.

What do you miss the most about your loved one(s)?

_____

_____

_____

_____

_____

_____

_____

_____

_____

_____

"Grief is not logical, rational, or anticipated. It strikes us unpredictably. For me, especially in the beginning, it felt like some days I was standing waist deep in the ocean as waves calmly slapped against my stomach in a steady ryhthm. But then there were days- sometimes minutes or hours- when suddenly the waves turned choppy, crashing and thrashing against me, and threatening to drag me under." ~Cathleeen Elle

Read more in her book *Shattered Together*

What are your waves like today?

_____

_____

_____

_____

_____

_____

_____

_____

_____

_____

_____

"There is no greater gift you can give someone in grief that to ask them about their loved one, and then truly listen. When we see our sorrow in the eyes of another, we know our grief has meaning. We get a glimpse, maybe for the first time since the loss, that we will survive, and a future is possible." –David Kessler

Read more in his book, *Finding Meaning The Sixth Stage of Grief.*

What was the absolute worst piece of advice someone gave you about grieving?

_____

_____

_____

_____

_____

_____

_____

_____

_____

_____

_____

"When the body is shed and we cross over to the spirit world, we open the door to eternal life. It is there that we discover that we are spiritual beings having human experiences." –James Van Praagh

Find out more in his book, *Healing Grief Reclaiming Life After Any Loss*

Write a love letter to your loved one. Tell them everything that you loved about them.

_____

_____

_____

_____

_____

_____

_____

_____

_____

_____

_____

_____

"What does meaning look like? It can take many shapes, such as finding gratitude for the time they had with loved ones, or finding ways to commemorate and honor loved ones, or realizing the brevity and value of life and making that the springboard into some kind of major shift or change." –David Kessler

Read more in his book, *Finding Meaning The Sixth Stage of Grief*

Write about the legacy your loved one left behind when they transitioned to spirit form. Share how you use this legacy in your life now.

_____

_____

_____

_____

_____

_____

_____

_____

_____

_____

"I often teach that in grief, pain is inevitable, but suffering is optional." ~David Kessler

Read more in his book, *Finding Meaning The Sixth Stage of Grief*

I really, really missed you today when....

_____

_____

_____

_____

_____

_____

_____

_____

_____

_____

_____

_____

"Shadow grief is 'a dull ache in the background of one's feelings that remains fairly constant and that, under certain circumstances and on certain occasions, comes bubbling to the surface, sometimes in the form of tears, sometimes not, but always accompanied by a feeling of sadness and a mild sense of anxiety." – Patrick O'Malley PHD with Tim Madigan

Read more in their book, *Getting Grief Right Finding Your Story of Love in the Sorrow of Loss*

Since you have been gone...

_____

_____

_____

_____

_____

_____

_____

_____

_____

_____

_____

_____

""Anguish is an almost unbearable and traumatic swirl of shock, incredulity, grief, and powerlessness." ~Brene Brown

Read more in her book, *The Atlas of the Heart.*

Write about the day you found out your loved one died.

"Heaven truly is a state and not a place. Our 'true home' is a way of being and not a location." ~Anita Moorjani

Read more in her book, *Dying to be Me.*

I wish I had told you....

_____

_____

_____

_____

_____

_____

_____

_____

_____

_____

_____

_____

"When the voice of regret is all you can hear, let the voice of love speak louder. If you find yourself consumed with guilt, remember that all has been forgiven." –Monica Ten-Kate

Read more in her book, *Monica the Medium Messages from Above*

I'm so sorry about....

_____

_____

_____

_____

_____

_____

_____

_____

_____

_____

_____

_____

""One of the main reasons Spirit comes through is because they love those of us here in the physical world so much that they want to help us move forward so that we can live the most joyful and fulfilling life possible...They want to support you in Heaven."
~Monica Ten-Kate

Read more in her book, *Monica the Medium Messages from Above*.

I wish I had been there when you transitioned to Spirit.
 OR
I'm glad I was by your side when you transitioned to Spirit.

_____

_____

_____

_____

_____

_____

_____

_____

_____

_____

"The definition of coincidence found in the American Heritage Dictionary is 'A sequence of events that although accidental seems to have been planned or arranged.' This definition, of course, begs the question, 'Planned or arranged by whom?' Most people answer, 'By God, that's who.' Whatever you call the creative life force, it seems to be not just an architect of the past but of the very minute-by-minute present of our lives." ~Squire Rushnell

Read more in Squire's book, *When God Winks at You.*

Thank you for the sign. I know it was you.

"You cannot control what happens to you in life, but you can always control what you feel and do about what happens to you." ~Viktor E. Frankl

Read more in his book, *Man's Search for Meaning.*

I need some advice. What do you think about....

_____

_____

_____

_____

_____

_____

_____

_____

_____

_____

_____

"You are a spiritual being. You are energy, and energy cannot be created or destroyed-it just changes form. Therefore, the pure essence of you has always been and always will be." ~ Rhonda Byrne

Read more in her book, *The Secret*.

I wish you knew about....

_____

_____

_____

_____

_____

_____

_____

_____

_____

_____

_____

_____

"But my mind clung to my wife's image, imagining it with an uncanny acuteness. I heard her answering me, saw her smile, her frank and encouraging look. Real or not, her look was then more luminous than the sun which was beginning to rise." –Vikto E. Frankl

Read more in his book, *Man's Search for Meaning*.

If I could have one more day with you, I would love to ....

_____

_____

_____

_____

_____

_____

_____

_____

_____

_____

""You can either stand still and live in yesterday or step through the gates of possibility into the life you were truly meant to live."~Brendan Bouchard

Read more in his book, *Life's Golden Ticket A Story About Second Chances.*

I understand there is a reason I am still here and you aren't. I'm going to use your memory to....

_____

_____

_____

_____

_____

_____

_____

_____

_____

_____

_____

_____

_____

""We run from grief because loss scares us, yet our hearts reach toward grief because the broken parts want to mend." ~Brene Brown

Read more in her book, *Rising Strong*.

Grief showed up today. I greeted it with open arms. Here is what happened.

_____

_____

_____

_____

_____

_____

_____

_____

_____

_____

_____

"Most of us want to believe that consciousness can continue after bodily death. When my father died, I began to explore if that is even possible. But wanting to believe something, even with all of your heart, doesn't make it true. As a sciency girl, I need evidence, and that's exactly what my story is all about." ~ Elizabeth Enton

Find out more about Liz's story in her book, *WTF Just Happened.*

I went to see a Medium today. Here is what happened.

"This moment was almost always the turning point for my clients as well-the moment when they came to understand that their grief was a function of their love." ~Patrick O'Malley PHD with Tim Madigan

Read more in their book, *Getting Grief Right Finding Your Story of Love in the Sorrow of Loss*

Why does it hurt so much? I know why....it was because of the depth of my love for you. Here is what my heart feels today.

_____

_____

_____

_____

_____

_____

_____

_____

_____

_____

_____

The following are blank pages to use however you choose.
Happy writing!

My wish for you is that you may you find peace each and every day. ~Monica

"Wherever you are on this journey, whatever path you choose to take, may you find peace, love, and a deeper connection to the world, your Self, and your loved one. Take your journey one hour at a time. Create a healing journey, not a story of pain.
You deserve it."
~Cathleen Elle
from
Shattered Together

Resources

Albom, M. (2018). The first phone call from heaven. Ulvercroft.

Burchard, B. (2016). Life's golden ticket: A story about second chances. HarperOne.

Byrne, R., & Byrne, R. (2006). Secret, the. Atria Books.

DeLong, P. D. (2019). I can see clearly now: A memoir about love, grief, and gratitude. Peacock Proud Press.

EATON, B. A. R. R. Y. (2016). Afterlife: Uncovering the secrets of life after death readhowyouwant.

Frankl, V. E., Kushner, H. S., & Winslade, W. J. (2006). Man's search for meaning. Beacon Press.

Kessler, D. (2020). Finding meaning: The sixth stage of grief. Scribner.

Konigsberg, R. D. (2011). The truth about grief: The myth of its five stages and the new science of loss. Simon & Schuster.

Moorjani, A. (2016). What if this is heaven?: How I released my limiting beliefs and really started living. Hay House.

O'Malley, P., & Madigan, T. (2017). Getting grief right: Finding your story of love in the sorrow of loss. Sounds True, Inc.

Praagh, J. V. (2009). Healing grief: Reclaiming life after any loss. Piatkus.

Robinson, E. (2017). There are no goodbyes: Guidance and comfort from those who have passed. Hay House Inc.

Ten-Kate, M. (2019). Messages from above: What your loved ones in heaven want you to know. 444 Publishing, a division of Monica the Medium, Inc.